Hist Whist

and other poems
for children

E. E. Cummings

Hist Whist

and other poems for children

Illustrated by
David Calsada

Edited by

George J. Firmage

Liveright   New York   London

First Edition

Published simultaneously in Canada
by Stoddart Publishing, Toronto

ISBN 0-87140-640-3

Liveright Publishing Corporation, 500 Fifth Avenue,
New York, N.Y. 10110
W. W. Norton & Company Ltd., 37 Great Russell Street,
London WC1B 3NU

1 2 3 4 5 6 7 8 9 0

Contents

Editor's Note

Sixteen of the twenty poems chosen for this collection by the poet appeared in a privately printed edition of 500 copies entitled *16 Poèmes Enfantins* in January 1962. The complete selection and the illustrations especially prepared for this new edition are published here for the first time.

G.J.F.

Hist Whist

and other poems for children

1

O the sun comes up-up-up in the opening

sky(the all the
any merry every pretty each

bird sings birds sing
gay-be-gay because today's today)the
romp cries i and the me purrs

you and the gentle
who-horns says-does moo-woo
(the prance with the
three white its stimpstamps)

the grintgrunt wugglewiggle
champychumpchomps yes
the speckled strut begins to scretch and
scratch-scrutch

and scritch(while
the no-she-yes-he fluffies tittle
tattle did-he-does-she)& the

ree ray rye roh
rowster shouts

rawrOO

2

in Just-
spring   when the world is mud-
luscious the little
lame balloonman

whistles   far   and wee

and eddieandbill come
running from marbles and
piracies and it's
spring

when the world is puddle-wonderful

the queer
old balloonman whistles
far   and   wee
and bettyandisbel come dancing

from hop-scotch and jump-rope and

it's
spring
and
      the

            goat-footed

balloonMan   whistles
far
and
wee

3

sentinel robins two
guard me and you
and little house this our
from hate from fear

a which of slim of blue
of here will who
straight up into the where
so safe we are

4

maggie and milly and molly and may
went down to the beach(to play one day)

and maggie discovered a shell that sang
so sweetly she couldn't remember her troubles,and

milly befriended a stranded star
whose rays five languid fingers were;

and molly was chased by a horrible thing
which raced sideways while blowing bubbles:and

may came home with a smooth round stone
as small as a world and as large as alone.

For whatever we lose(like a you or a me)
it's always ourselves we find in the sea

5

if everything happens that can't be done
(and anything's righter
than books
could plan)
the stupidest teacher will almost guess
(with a run
skip
around we go yes)
there's nothing as something as one

one hasn't a why or because or although
(and buds know better
than books
don't grow)
one's anything old being everything new
(with a what
which
around we come who)
one's everyanything so

so world is a leaf so tree is a bough
(and birds sing sweeter
than books
tell how)
so here is away and so your is a my
(with a down
up
around again fly)
forever was never till now

now i love you and you love me
(and books are shuter
than books
can be)

and deep in the high that does nothing but fall
(with a shout
each
around we go all)
there's somebody calling who's we

we're anything brighter than even the sun
(we're everything greater
than books
might mean)
we're everyanything more than believe
(with a spin
leap
alive we're alive)
we're wonderful one times one

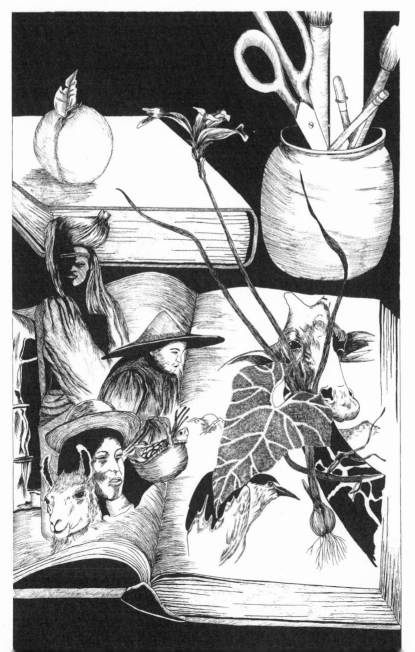

6

the little horse is newlY

Born)he knows nothing,and feels
everything;all around whom is

perfectly a strange
ness(Of sun
light and of fragrance and of

Singing)is ev
erywhere(a welcom
ing dream:is amazing)
a worlD.and in

this world lies:smoothbeautifuL
ly folded;a(brea
thing and a gro

Wing)silence,who;
is:somE

oNe.

7

for any ruffian of the sky
your kingbird doesn't give a damn—
his royal warcry is I AM
and he's the soul of chivalry

in terror of whose furious beak
(as sweetly singing creatures know)
cringes the hugest heartless hawk
and veers the vast most crafty crow

your kingbird doesn't give a damn
for murderers of high estate
whose mongrel creed is Might Makes Right
—his royal warcry is I AM

true to his mate his chicks his friends
he loves because he cannot fear
(you see it in the way he stands
and looks and leaps upon the air)

8

& sun &

sil
e
nce
e

very

w
here
noon
e

is exc

ep
t
on
t

his

b
oul
der
a

drea(chipmunk)ming

9

now(more near ourselves than we)
is a bird singing in a tree,
who never sings the same thing twice
and still that singing's always his

eyes can feel but ears may see
there never lived a gayer he;
if earth and sky should break in two
he'd make them one(his song's so true)

who sings for us for you for me
for each leaf newer than can be:
and for his own(his love)his dear
he sings till everywhere is here

10

o by the by
has anybody seen
little you-i
who stood on a green
hill and threw
his wish at blue

with a swoop and a dart
out flew his wish
(it dived like a fish
but it climbed like a dream)
throbbing like a heart
singing like a flame

blue took it my
far beyond far
and high beyond high
bluer took it your
but bluest took it our
away beyond where

what a wonderful thing
is the end of a string
(murmurs little you-i
as the hill becomes nil)
and will somebody tell
me why people let go

11

hist   whist
little ghostthings
tip-toe
twinkle-toe

little twitchy
witches and tingling
goblins
hob-a-nob   hob-a-nob

little hoppy happy
toad in tweeds
tweeds
little itchy mousies

with scuttling
eyes   rustle and run   and
hidehidehide
whisk

whisk   look out for the old woman
with the wart on her nose
what she'll do to yer
nobody knows

for she knows the devil   ooch
the devil   ouch
the devil
ach   the great

green
dancing
devil
devil

devil
devil

        wheeEEE

12

why did you go
little fourpaws?
you forgot to shut
your big eyes.

where did you go?
like little kittens
are all the leaves
which open in the rain.

little kittens who
are called spring,
is what we stroke
maybe asleep?

do you know?or maybe did
something go away
ever so quietly
when we weren't looking.

13

mouse)Won
derfully is
anyone else entirely who doesn't
move(Moved more suddenly than)whose

tiniest smile?may Be
bigger than the fear of all
hearts never which have
(Per

haps)loved(or than
everyone that will Ever love)we
've
hidden him in A leaf

and,
Opening
beautiful earth
put(only)a Leaf among dark

ness.sunlight's
thenlike?now
Disappears
some

thing(silent:
madeofimagination
;the incredible soft)ness
(his ears(eyes

14

!

o(rounD)moon,how
do
you(rouNd
er
than roUnd)float;
who
lly &(rOunder than)
go
:ldenly(Round
est)

?

15

porky & porkie
sit into a moon)

blacker than dreams
are round like a spoon are
both making silence

two-made-of-one

& nothing tells anywhere
"snow will come soon" &
pretending they're birds sit

creatures of quills
(asleep who must go

things-without-wings

16

if a cheerfulest Elephantangelchild should sit

(holding a red candle over his head
by a finger of trunk,and singing out of a red

book)on a proud round cloud in a white high night

where his heartlike ears have flown adorable him
self tail and all(and his tail's red christmas bow)
—and if,when we meet again,little he(having flown
even higher)is sunning his penguinsoul in the glow

of a joy which wasn't and isn't and won't be words

while possibly not(at a guess)quite half way down
to the earth are leapandswooping tinily birds
whose magical gaiety makes your beautiful name—

i feel that(false and true are merely to know)
Love only has ever been,is,and will ever be,So

17

who are you,little i

(five or six years old)
peering from some high

window;at the gold

of november sunset

(and feeling:that if day
has to become night

this is a beautiful way)

18

blossoming are people

nimbler than Really
go whirling into gaily

white thousands return

by millions and dreaming

drift hundreds come swimming
(Each a keener secret

than silence even tells)

all the earth has turned to sky

are flowers neither why nor how
when is now and which is Who

and i am you are i am we

(pretty twinkle merry bells)

Someone has been born
everyone is noone

dance around the snowman

19

who(is?are)who

(two faces at a dark
window)this father and his
child are watching snowflakes
(falling & falling & falling)

eyes eyes

looking(alw
ays)while
earth and sky grow
one with won

der until(see

the)with the
bigger much than biggest
(little is)now(dancing yes for)white
ly(joy!joy!joy)and whiteliest all

wonderings are silence is becom

ing each
truebeautifully
more-than-thing
(& falling &)

EverychildfatheringOne

20

little tree
little silent Christmas tree
you are so little
you are more like a flower

who found you in the green forest
and were you very sorry to come away?
see   i will comfort you
because you smell so sweetly

i will kiss your cool bark
and hug you safe and tight
just as your mother would,
only don't be afraid

look   the spangles
that sleep all the year in a dark box
dreaming of being taken out and allowed to shine,
the balls the chains red and gold the fluffy threads,

put up your little arms
and i'll give them all to you to hold
every finger shall have its ring
and there won't be a single place dark or unhappy

then when you're quite dressed
you'll stand in the window for everyone to see
and how they'll stare!
oh but you'll be very proud

and my little sister and i will take hands
and looking up at our beautiful tree
we'll dance and sing
"Noel Noel"